Victorian
Sentimental
Jewellery

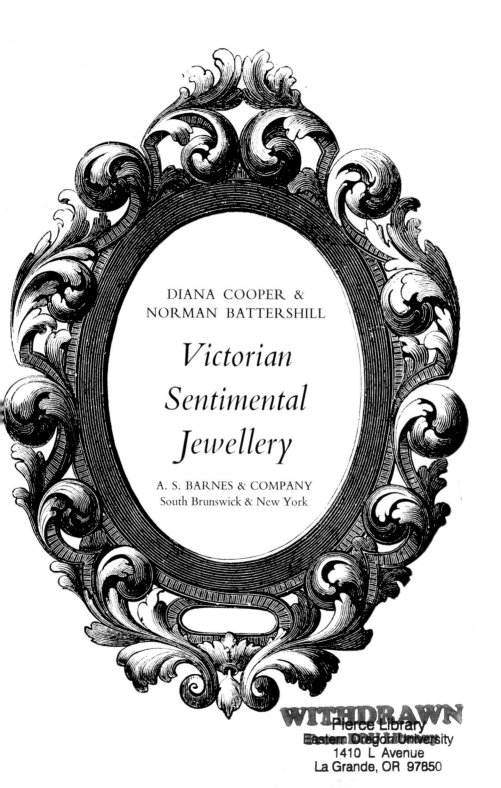

DIANA COOPER &
NORMAN BATTERSHILL

Victorian

Sentimental

Jewellery

A. S. BARNES & COMPANY
South Brunswick & New York

ISBN 0-498-01261-1

Library of Congress Catalogue Card Number: 72-5877

Printed in Great Britain

Contents

Note

Except where otherwise stated, the reproductions which follow are twice actual size.

Foreword

Every mood or diversion in the progress of civilisation has been reflected in the artistry of the age. Jewellery, perhaps more than any, shows the sharp changes, gradual digressions and rise and fall in social and economic conditions throughout history, for the jeweller is concerned with commerce as well as creation. Design has to match demand.

Each period produces its own representative design in jewellery. We recognise the flamboyance of the Elizabethans, the intricacies and flippancies of the French court in the eighteenth century and the more classical and restrained approach of the Georgian age in Britain.

Until the nineteenth century the wearing of jewellery was largely confined to the wealthier classes but in Victorian times the use of machinery began to replace hand craftsmanship. With the use of cheaper materials it became possible for the workshops to produce decorative pieces within the reach of the middle class and, towards the end of the Victorian era, also for the working class. Silver to some extent replaced gold, and ivory, coral, bog oak and jet, which could be turned and carved, were increasingly used for making popular jewellery which reflected the attitudes of the day—sentimental love, the solidarity of the family and a preoccupation with mourning for those who had 'passed on'. The code of mourning was strict and it was not until after the Silver Jubilee of 1887 that there was some relaxation. This led to the enormous popularity of the silver love brooch. This book deals with sentimental jewellery throughout the reign of Queen Victoria.

7

I
MOURNING JEWELLERY

Introductory

Although mourning for the dead reached its peak in Victorian times, public and private mourning was already common in the seventeenth century. When Charles I was executed in 1649 many of his subjects wore rings or brooches with the letters CR engraved upon them, and members of a family often wore death's head jewellery when a relative died.

In the eighteenth century poets like Edward Young and Thomas Gray wrote poems about death. Young's elegy 'On the Death of Queen Anne' (1713) and his 'Night Thoughts of Life, Death and Immortality' (1742–4) reflected the feelings people had about death and the after-life. Gray's 'Elegy written in a Country Churchyard' (1750) was greeted in all levels of society as an expression of the prevailing attitude towards the sadness of old age and death. At this period the wearing of mourning jewellery among the wealthier classes was quite usual. It was common to wear a pendant or brooch containing a lock of hair from the loved one who had died. Even rings were made so that a small plait of hair could be enclosed. In the early nineteenth century mourning had already become a ritual. When His Royal Highness the Duke of York died in 1827 the Earl Marshal issued an order which stated:

> . . . upon the present melancholy occasion of the death of the late Royal Highness Frederick Duke of York and Albany, next brother to His Majesty, it is expected that all persons do put themselves into deep mourning.

The fashion magazines at once produced illustrations with suitable costumes. Dinner dresses were of black silk or bombazine accompanied by 'bracelets, necklace and earrings of jet' (1).

1 *Fashion plate of mourning dress from the* Ladies Monthly
Magazine, *February 1827*

Ten years later, when Queen Victoria came to the throne during the period of mourning for William IV, she inherited an established code of mourning which became increasingly significant in social life during her long reign. Whatever else may be said about the Victorians, they pursued their aims with a singular strength of purpose and paid great attention to detail in pursuit of conformity and respectability. Preoccupation with family solidarity and with comfort in death became a major factor in their lives for they approached all the various attentions to well-being and romanticism with vigour. From this evolved a unity of style which was to last well into the twentieth century.

The ritual which followed death became increasingly elaborate in the third quarter of the nineteenth century when mourning was carried to fantastic extremes, largely owing to the example set by Queen Victoria after the death of the Prince Consort in 1861. Already in the 1850s the funeral of a relative was a matter for major concern. A great deal of money and effort was expended in staging a first-class spectacle which, as the catalogue of the Great Exhibition of 1851 records, might include a lead coffin and outside case, hearse and four horses, two coaches and pairs with plumes and equipment of superior description.

2 (above left) *Heart-shaped pendant in jet carved with roses and forget-me-nots*
3 (above right) *Bible pendant in carved jet*
4 (below left) *Pear-shaped pendant in jet carved with roses, forget-me-nots and a thistle*
5 (below right) *Oval locket in carved jet with floral decoration*

The dresses and jewellery worn matched the occasion. For the wealthy a fine funeral was a symbol of status and the poor tried to emulate the rich so that many a humble purse was stretched to its limit and beyond to attain a similar cortege.

In Victorian times life was hard for the poor and it was sometimes a comfort to be able to believe in a future life which would be some compensation for the drudgery and deprivations of life on earth. Emotional compensation was also a factor. A fine funeral sometimes helped to solve the consciences of relatives who may not have behaved too well towards the deceased in his or her lifetime. A Victorian music-hall song expresses this remorse which needed to be expiated . . .

> . . . Dead! they had parted in anger.
> Dead? and he could not know
> How bitterly she had repented
> The words that had vexed him so.
> That moment a heart was broken
> Alas for the love links riven!
> Alas for the words unspoken!
> And the kiss that was never given.

The love, whether sincerely felt or not, must thus be expressed in mourning. The period of mourning after a funeral involved the wearing of black dresses and mourning jewellery on all occasions.

6 (above) *Jet hand-brooch carved with roses, forget-me-nots and yew*
7 (below) *Jet brooch carved to resemble branched coral further decorated with a jet chair and cross*

In 1850 Queen Victoria, when mourning the death of the Duke of Clarence, attended banquets in a black silk dress wearing jet jewellery. The periods of full and half mourning could extend over a period of two years. When one recalls the high mortality rate of the period, particularly among infants, and the military casualties suffered in the 1850s in the Indian Mutiny and the Crimean War, it is obvious that some women could spend years of their lives in mourning. Indeed, it became so much of a habit that elderly ladies continued to use black bombazine as their main dress material even when not in mourning.

After the death of Prince Albert, Queen Victoria imposed on herself the most stringent discipline in mourning which was continued with little relief for the rest of her life and was widely followed by her subjects. There was little relaxation until after the Silver Jubilee of 1887, when the sentimental love brooch became fashionable.

Design in mourning jewellery received the same amount of attention as the splendid funeral occasions. Even the humblest pendants and brooches show some originality of design and there are many examples of fine craftsmanship. Jet was the main material used for mourning jewellery and to meet the enormous demand a large and flourishing industry grew up on the Yorkshire coast in and around the little fishing port of Whitby.

8   (above) *Oval brooch in polished jet carrying a gold serpent with tongue to tail*

9   (below) *Bracelet with jet medallion carved with roses*

The History of Whitby Jet

Jet is a form of fossilised driftwood found in the bituminous shales of the Upper Lias rocks of the Yorkshire coast between Robin Hood's Bay and Boulby, just north of Starthes. It has been used to make ornaments since the Bronze Age for beads of jet have been found buried with skeletons in local barrows of the period. Rings made of jet have also been found in Roman sites. A number of early writers including Solinus, Bede and Camillus Leonardus refer to jet or 'black amber' in Britain, and Camden translated a verse by Leonardus which recognises the peculiar property it possesses of attracting to it, when rubbed, light dry objects:

> Peat stone, almost a gem, the Lybians find,
> But fruitful Britain sends a wondrous kind;
> 'Tis black and shining, smooth and ever bright;
> 'Twill draw up straws if rubbed till hot and bright.

Remains of rosary beads and crucifixes have been found in the ruins of Whitby Abbey and may now be seen in Whitby Museum. All these early examples of jet were fashioned entirely by hand.

In 1622 Michael Drayton refers to jet in his *Polyolbion*, a topographical description of England:

> . . . The rocks of Moulgrace, too, my glories forth to set,
> Out of their crannied cleeves, can give you perfect jet.

The Rise of the Victorian Jet Industry

The reefs of shale containing jet occur not only in the cliffs of the Yorkshire coast but also extend under the sea. As these submarine reefs are eroded, jet is washed up along the shore as far afield as Saltburn in the north and Bridlington in the south. This 'washed jet' was collected for use in the workshops of Whitby to supplement the jet dug from shallow workings in the Cleveland Hills at such centres as Bilsdale. Most pieces of jet are quite small. The finest piece of rough jet ever found weighed only 11¼lb. It was 6ft 4in long, 4½in wide and 1½in thick. Examples of unworked jet may be seen in the Whitby Museum.

The first use of machinery to work jet was in the early years of the nineteenth century when Captain Treulett, a naval pensioner living in Whitby, is said to have succeeded in turning amber and jet beads and by passing on his skill started the jet industry. In 1808 he instructed John Carter, an innkeeper of Haggersgate and Robert Jefferson, a painter, in his methods and they became the first two makers of commercial jet jewellery. They employed a turner, Matthew Hill, and the business slowly expanded. By 1832 there were two jet workshops in the town with some twenty-five workers. By 1850 the number of workshops had increased to seven including that of Thomas Andrews of New Quay who became 'jet ornament maker to H.M. Queen Victoria'. In the following year jet jewellery was displayed at the Great Exhibition in London and as a result orders began to pour in. In 1854 the Queen of Bavaria sent to Isaac Greenberg of Baxtergate, Whitby, for a jet cable-chain guard 4ft 6in long. Greenberg also sent bracelets to the Empress of France. An export trade in jet had begun.

12 *The jet works of William Wright of Haggersgate and Marine Parade, Whitby, c1875. This was the only jet works at this period to use lathes power driven by gas engines; the others used treadle wheels. This picture is of special interest because it was taken by F. M. Sutcliffe (1853–1941), a pioneer Whitby photographer who gained an international reputation for his studies of local people and local scenes. These brought him awards in exhibitions all over the world and an Honorary Fellowship of the Royal Photographic Society*

After the death of Prince Albert in 1861 the demand for jet ornamental jewellery both at home and abroad reached a peak. By 1870 1,500 men, women and children were employed in the industry which maintained over 100 dealers and manufacturers in Whitby as well as some workshops in Scarborough. Among the many workers attracted to jet-making there proved to be a number of craftsmen capable of producing wares of the most beautiful form and workmanship. Very high wages were paid even to the crudest hands, many of whom were only part-time workers.

The workers who carved and engraved jet tended to specialise as they developed their skill. Some carved in relief perhaps concentrating on flowers or portrait medallions; others found it more congenial to engrave designs on the polished surface of the jet. Sometimes a single brooch would have both carved and incised work, passing from one craftsman to another.

Unfortunately, the outstanding craftsmen did not as a rule sign their work. It is possible, however, to see authentic examples of the work of a number of artists in the Whitby Museum. E. H. Greenbury, perhaps the most skilful of them all, who had a shop in what is now known as Dock End, won the medal and Freedom of the Worshipful Company of Turners. Two jet caskets he designed and made for the Philadelphia International Exhibition of 1876, decorated with busts and medallions, may be seen in St Thomas's Museum, Scarborough, and there is a jet clock case made by Greenbury in the Museum of Archaeology and Bygones at Scarborough.

13 (above) *Jet ear-rings with pendulums which swing through the main design*
14 (below) *Spherical ear-rings of polished jet with chains of small jet links (The original hooks have been replaced)*

H. Barraclough, who was for some years conductor of the Whitby Saloon Band, was noted for carving fruit and foliage. Other well-known artists included W. H. Crane, Isaac Greenbury, Thomas Jose, T. Kraggs and W. Lund. A brooch or pendant signed with the initials of any of these men would be of very special interest to a collector.

Much detailed information about the jet industry including a list of the larger firms making jet jewellery is contained in an excellent booklet by Hugh P. Kendall, formerly Curator of the Whitby Museum: *The Story of Whitby Jet: Its Workers from Earliest Times.*

Unfortunately for the town of Whitby the boom in mourning jewellery lasted little more than twenty years. By 1884 fewer than 300 workers remained. By 1921 there were only 40 workers, many part-timers who met the intermittent demand. Matthew Snowden, the last of the jet craftsmen died in 1932 at the age of seventy-five. The decline in the industry was only partly due to changes in fashion. Competition from cheaper materials also played a part. Black glass, often known as French jet (15), began to replace true jet and new synthetic materials such as ebonite and vulcanite were also used. Efforts were made to restrict the use of these materials but without much success. Today such products are sold in Whitby correctly labelled as 'simulated jet'.

15 (above) *Jet locket carved with a single rose*
16 (below) *Jet strung on an elastic thread to form a serpent bracelet*

Other Materials Used in Mourning Jewellery

It is fairly easy for the collector to distinguish between true jet and French jet. Whitby jet is warmer, softer and less likely to fracture under impact than French jet. It is relatively easy to turn, carve or engrave. French jet is black glass and has the brittle quality of glass. It is shiny when polished and the decoration is normally cut. French pieces may include cameos. The large brooch of French jet (17), mounted on brass, is a fine example of its kind but close examination will reveal small chips on the edges. The classical Grecian figure represents sorrow weeping at the funeral urn. The surround is faceted which increases the reflection of light. Queen Victoria was very fond of cameos and her tastes invariably extended to the court and thence to the general public.

Bog oak is a dark brown wood, similar in appearance to jet, found in the peat deposits of Ireland. It has been used from time to time for inlay work since the sixteenth century, but enjoyed a revival after attention had been drawn to it in the Great Exhibition of 1851. It was then much used for mourning and religious pieces, particularly in Ireland. Traditional folk jewellery is often worn to confirm allegiance and patriotism to one's country and the pride that people took in their homeland. Bog oak was therefore more appropriate for use in Ireland than Whitby jet.

17 (above) *Oval cameo brooch in French jet*
18 (below left) *Crucifix pendant in bog oak with a central anchor*
19 (below right) *Crucifix pendant in bog oak carved with flowers*

C

The carved examples of bog oak (18 and 19) show particularly good workmanship. Most bog oak jewellery dates from between 1850 and 1885, though some carvings have been made since that date to meet a demand from the tourist industry.

Tortoiseshell was occasionally used for mourning jewellery with inlaid decoration of gold or silver after the fashion of Castellani. The work is known as piqué and was introduced to England from France by the refugee Huguenots in the seventeenth century. The crucifix (20) which is inlaid with gold and silver flowers dates from about 1860. Mass production began in Birmingham in 1872 after which geometrical designs became popular on crosses and brooches.

The import of tortoiseshell has never been great, just sufficient to keep a few workshops supplied. The best shell comes from the Hawkbill Turtle, one of the smaller species about $3\frac{1}{2}$ft across and weighing under 100lb. They are found mainly along the Pacific coast of South and Central America and on the Atlantic coast of South America and the USA as far as Massachusetts. A few are found on the west coast of Africa and stragglers have been found in the Orkney Islands.

Ivory has always been acceptable on mourning jewellery. It is mainly used for carved decoration as on the brooch of polished jet (21) which carries a spray of acorns, the symbol of a long life ended.

20 (above) *Tortoiseshell crucifix with piqué work in gold and silver*
21 (below) *Jet brooch decorated with oak leaves and acorns in carved ivory*

The quality of ivory varies greatly. The best, which comes from the tusks of African elephants, retains a fine white appearance and is more costly than Asian ivory which has a yellow appearance. A number of other materials are sometimes referred to as ivory—the teeth of hippopotami, the teeth of the sperm whale, the bones of animals and the seeds of certain types of palm trees. Plastics and celluloid also masquerade as ivory from time to time though few people are deceived by synthetic materials.

Black enamel was used on mourning jewellery over a long period, especially for brooches (22–25) and rings (26–29), sometimes with coloured enamels. Enamel is made from a glassy material and the colours are obtained by the addition of various metallic oxides in powder form. The enamel is fused to a metal base at high temperature.

The metals used in mourning jewellery are usually either an alloy of gold, an alloy of other metals made to resemble gold, or a base metal that has been gilded to resemble gold. Early Victorian jewellery used either 22 or 18 carat gold, but in 1854 three lower standards were allowed—15, 12 and 9 carat. This made it possible to make a considerable reduction in price and to open up a larger market. It is worth noting that the 15 and 12 carat standards were replaced in 1932 by a new 14 carat gold.

22 (above left) *Black enamel brooch with scrolls of gold filigree finishing in narrow leaves set with pearls*

23 (above right) *Heart-shaped pendant in gold and black enamel with convolvulus and forget-me-nots inlaid in gold*

24 (below left) *Black enamel brooch on an alloy base framed in scrolls of gold*

25 (below right) *Gold and enamel brooch with hand-painted forget-me-nots*

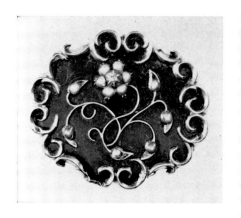

Rolled gold consists of a layer of gold fused to a less expensive metal such as bronze or silver and then rolled into a thin sheet.

Pinchbeck is a material that looks remarkably like gold. It was invented by a London watchmaker, Christopher Pinchbeck, early in the eighteenth century and consists of copper with a small proportion of zinc. It keeps its colour when worn and was widely used for well over 100 years. However, its use declined after 1854 when 9 carat gold became available.

It is not always immediately possible to identify the metal used in a piece of jewellery unless a clear hallmark can be seen. If this is visible on gold or silver it will provide very useful information about the quality and age of a piece. A book of hallmarks and a magnifying glass are essential pieces of equipment when buying jewellery. The *Guide to Marks of Origin on British and Irish Silver Plate*, compiled by F. Bradbury and published by J. W. Northend Ltd of Sheffield, can be recommended as an invaluable pocket-book.

26 (above left) *Ring with shield-shaped centrepiece in gold and black enamel holding a small blue flower with green leaves (c1840)*

27 (above right) *Ring with heart-shaped centrepiece with a pearl set in black enamel. The words 'Never Forgotten' are engraved behind the heart (c1840)*

28 (below left) *Masculine gold ring with panels of black enamel. A name is engraved inside the ring with the date of death, 1863*

29 (below right) *Masculine ring in gold and black enamel with the words 'In Memory of' and engraved inside the inscription 'Mother Died Dec 30th. 1887'*

The less expensive gold alloys and gilded metals were used extensively with jet and particularly French jet. The jet ear-rings (30) have an unusual pinchbeck setting of large golden grains clustered much as Castellani had used in a design many years earlier. Ear-drops of this shape became popular after Adelina Patti, the singer, appeared in whole parures of jet balls and beads in 1867, including necklace, ear-rings, brooch and bracelets. The use of gold alloys or gilding with French jet is seen mainly in brooches (31, 32, 33) where the gold provides ornamentation and often a frame for the small plaits of hair so frequently found in mourning jewellery (see pp 43–51). The great disadvantage of French jet is its liability to chip if dropped or knocked against some hard object (31).

More elaborate pieces were often produced by using pierced metal or by decorating with gold wire to give a lacy appearance. Such brooches were often decorated with seed pearls which were symbolic of tears. Pearls were sometimes used with white enamel after the death of an unmarried person.

30 (above left) *Polished jet ear-rings in heavy teardrop shapes with a pinchbeck setting*

31 (above right) *Rectangular brooch of French jet on a brass base on which a small gold frame with a pattern of roses holds plaited hair*

32 (below left) *Brooch of faceted French jet mounted on a good quality alloy holding an oval gold frame for plaited hair*

33 (below right) *Oval brooch of cut and polished French jet with gilt scrollwork and frame for plaited hair*

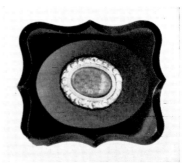

Hair Jewellery

Hair jewellery was common in Georgian times and its use continued throughout the reign of Queen Victoria and was particularly in vogue after about 1850. The Victorians seemed to find a lasting comfort in the memories which were held in a physically personal memento. The commonest items of hair jewellery were the brooch and the locket. These usually have a central frame or medallion with plaited hair and often carry the name or initials of the deceased.

In 1858 the French fashion magazine *La Belle Assemblé* refers to the jewellery of Limmoniér 'in which some beloved tress or precious curl is entwined'. The plaiting and preparation of the hair was a professional job and many hair artists in England and France maintained businesses based on this craft. Fosser of Hanover Street, Cleal of Poland Street and Bakewell of Red Lion Street were well known and showed their work at exhibitions. Such displays were usually impersonal in approach and the human hair was worked with horsehair to give it a firmer finish. Gold wire thread was often coiled into the composition and small pearls added.

34 (above left) *Late Victorian oval brooch of French jet and pierced gold with a frame for plaited hair surrounded by small pearls*

35 (above right) *Filigree pinchbeck frame for plaited hair, decorated with pearls*

36 (below left) *Gilt alloy frame decorated with leaves, containing hair arranged by an amateur*

37 (below right) *Circular gold locket with hair of two colours, bound by pearls. The reverse side carries the words 'In Memory of' in black enamel*

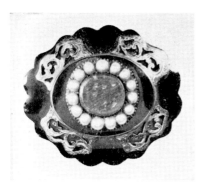

Many different pieces, plaited and woven, finished in gold with clasps, buckles and fittings were shown, and some have survived. Glue was used for stiffening and also to fix the hair when mounted on watered silk or against an enamel or opal glass background. Apart from this only tweezers, knife and curling iron, patience and imagination, and some manual dexterity were required.

Not all mourners could afford to employ top-line artists and much hairwork was done by amateurs, usually by the daughters of the house who found instructions in manuals such as Alexanna Speight's *Lock of Hair* (1891). The work, however, was often badly done (36).

The words 'In Memory of' are often found on mourning jewellery, sometimes in Gothic lettering (38, 60) and sometimes with sanserif (40–43). This became very popular between 1850 and 1860. They can often be dated from an inscription (39, 40).

Monogrammed jewellery sometimes included the initials of a widow's christian name as well as the entwined initials of the deceased husband's names (38). One brooch illustrated (40) has two inscriptions—'R. Morrell. Died Oct 22 1859' and 'R. Morrell died Nov 7th 1914'. The sentimental value of this brooch clearly spanned two generations.

38 (above left) *Dark tortoiseshell brooch with gold and silver initials, c1870*

39 (above right) *Dual purpose hair brooch/pendant in gold and black enamel, c1839*

40 (centre left) *Hair brooch in gold and black enamel, c1859*

41 (centre right) *Hair brooch in gilt and black enamel*

42 (below left) *Hair brooch in black enamel with letters in silver*

43 (below right) *Gold locket inlaid with black enamel containing hair, the initials of the deceased and the date—1871.*

Lockets in which the hair was concealed (43) were as popular as the brooch in Victorian times. In 1858 a contemporary periodical stated that lockets and pendants 'could be worn by all ages' and in the 1870s they were probably the most favoured neckwear: the fashionable columns describe them as 'an indispensable finish to the toilet'. Nevertheless, brooches held their place and in the *Queen Magazine* in 1880 an article by Elaine de Marsay states that 'brooches are given this season in preference to lockets . . .'.

The custom of wearing mourning rings dates from the reign of Charles II and even in 1690 some were adapted to carry locks of hair. The Victorians plaited the hair and it was carried in a tiny frame which replaced the major gem or stone of the more usual type of ring. Sometimes the plait was placed behind the stone which opened outwards on a hinge (44).

A number of other types of mourning jewellery displayed hair, including tiepins in which the hair was kept in a small frame.

44 (above left) *A hair ring carrying a circle of black enamel set with a cross of pearls which opens to show a plait of hair under glass, c1870. The words engraved inside the band read* 'Joseph Payne. Died March 22 1870'

45 (above right) *Pinchbeck ring with heavy decorated shank, c1838. Engraved inside the band are the words HENRI LEGG, died May 5th 1838'*

46 (centre left) *Hair ring in gold and black enamel, c1848. The inscription inside the band reads* 'My dear Father: obit. 3rd July 1846. Ae 62'

47 (centre right) *Pinchbeck ring pave-set with garnets. An inset of hair is under glass at the back*

48 (below left) *Hair ring with silver filigree surround, bezel setting and a single cut garnet. The centre opens on a delicate hinge revealing hair beneath glass*

49 (below right) *Hair ring with the frame surrounded by almandine garnets*

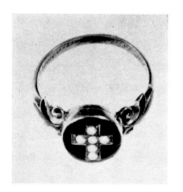

D

49

Long lengths of human hair from the deceased were sometimes skilfully woven to form a bracelet (51) or even a 'cord' which could be used for a watch chain or ribbon (52). The taste for such work fluctuated. It appears to have grown in popularity in the 1840s and 1850s. The hair was used in several different ways and the craft became highly specialised. One of the major craftsmen was B. Lee of 41 Rathbone Place, London, who exhibited his work at the Great Exhibition of 1851. The hair was sometimes bound as ropework, and sometimes plaited into flat bands. Occasionally it was woven so that it would pass through a gilt buckle.

Alfred Shuff, of 34 Great Marlborough Street, London, was noted for hairwork and one of his gold-mounted bracelets dated 1865 may be seen in the London Museum. James Laver in *Victoriana* (1966) illustrates a pair of ear-rings made of hair (plate 151) and describes them as 'a strange and rather morbid by-product of the Victorian taste for mementoes of the dead'.

Although hairwork of this kind was mainly in vogue in mid-Victorian times, this type of 'jewellery' was still being worn as late as 1880.

50 (above) *'Cord' for a pocket watch woven from the hair of a deceased relative, with gold fittings*

51 (below) *Small bracelet of hair with embossed gold fitting and pendant heart*

Photographic Mementoes

The coming of photography saw the decline of hair jewellery. The small portraits known as daguerreotypes had been used as mementoes in mid-Victorian times, mounted in attractive cases which could be carried. Photography, however, was too complicated a business for the amateur until the introduction of the dry plate in the 1880s. From this time onwards small portrait photographs on paper became available and these were carried in brooches, lockets and pendants which were made to open. Sometimes the photographs were mounted behind glass for all to see (52). Lockets and pendants were made to open on a hinge to reveal a small frame, or sometimes two—one on either side. When the Eastman Kodak camera was launched in 1888 the family 'snap' became a part of social life. The size of brooches and lockets tended on average to increase in order to carry a reasonably large photograph. There is, as a rule, no difficulty in distinguishing a locket designed to hold hair from one made to take a photograph. The hair was intended to remain; the little photographic frame will normally open with ease. Moreover these were not used solely as mourning jewellery. They often contained the photographs of a living relative or a sweetheart.

52 (above) *Brooch with woven gold surround for a photograph frame. The frame is on a swivel and carries glass on both sides, c1890–1900*

53 (below) *Oval carved jet locket with the symbols of faith, hope and charity. The locket opens to reveal a glass frame on either side*

Relaxation of the Mourning Code

Twenty years of heavy mourning after the death of Prince Albert began to pall on the general public and even more so among the manufacturers of jewellery except, of course, the users of Whitby jet. As a result an approach was made to the Princess of Wales in 1885 to see if she could help to gain some relaxation of the code, but no reply was received. In the same year *The Ladies Treasury* reported: 'Nothing but dog collars are seen. These may be in plain or beaded velvet for ordinary mortals', but then continued to suggest diamonds for ladies of fashion. For mourning such collars were often made of French jet faceted to give the maximum sparkle under artificial light (54). Bracelets were also much favoured by those who began to turn away from heavy mourning. It was normal to wear two or three bracelets, but only a single one if in mourning to accentuate its significance. The black enamel was usually decorated with inlaid flowers. The lilies of the valley, for example, symbolise happiness in the hereafter, reflecting a more positive attitude to mourning (55).

In 1887, after 'certain delays' lasting two years, a reply was received to the letter sent to the Princess of Wales. This was the year of the Silver Jubilee and Queen Victoria had agreed to wear some silver jewellery on state occasions. At last the days of excessive mourning were over and the market was opened for a flood of silver sentimental jewellery which reflected a new attitude to love and family affection.

II
LOVE BROOCHES

Introductory

After the Silver Jubilee of 1887 when Queen Victoria relaxed some of her self-imposed mourning rules, the jet industry at Whitby, which was already in decline, slumped rapidly. The jewellery trade in silver, however, began to plan for expansion. In that year the Birmingham Jewellers' and Silversmiths' Association was formed and one of its first moves was to administer special training facilities. Forty promising students from the ages of twelve to twenty were enrolled at the Municipal School of Art in Birmingham for special training in artistic design work, and the Association agreed to pay half the fees involved. Interested employers, with a foresight often lacking in those days, were found to pay the other half and it may be said that, in spite of setbacks from time to time, the silver trade in its broader aspect took root and flourished from then on.

The trade in small silver pieces catered almost entirely for a home market, but during the mid-Victorian era some export developed to South America. This was later taken by the USA whose output was increasing, and eventually a high protective tariff (50 per cent in some cases) slowed down export from England altogether. Canada began to import from the United States and only at the end of the century did a little of the export market, this time to South Africa, pick up at all.

57 (above) *Silver brooch with scalloped and beaded edge, carrying a woven basket with gilded flowers and leaves which can be moved on stems of wire so that they fall gracefully over the edge of the ropework. Assayed in 1893*

58 (below) *An oval gold frame brooch decorated with ropework and a key pattern of black inlaid enamel. The brooch has a small ring attached so that it may, if desired, be used as a pendant*

In 1890 the duty that had hitherto applied to all gold articles of 18 carat and 22 carat and to all silver ware was abolished. The relief given by this tax concession led to the start of a 'trinket trade', and small pieces of sentimental jewellery began to find their level of popularity. Very soon these became the trade's lifeline, reaching a peak with the death of Queen Victoria in 1901, which itself created a demand for mementoes and commemorative symbols.

The most popular of all the inexpensive items of jewellery that flooded the market was the silver love brooch which was within the purse of all but the very poor. The manufacture of these brooches and trinkets was fairly simple. The parts of a silver ornament were cut to shape by presses and the decoration was put on in a stamp. If more than one part was involved, the parts were assembled and soldered together. In some cases a little hand-engraving was done or areas were left plain so that the retailer could arrange for special names or designs to be engraved to meet the wishes of the individual customers. The range of designs was enormous and many of the love brooches show great individuality. The shapes and decoration were often symbolic. Judged by modern standards they are excessively sentimental but they faithfully expressed the attitudes of late Victorian days, attitudes which persisted until World War I.

59 (above) *Silver name brooch in which the fret-cut letters are decorated with linked leaves and flowers (actual size)*

60 (below) *Fret-cut silver brooch with the initials of the owner— B.C.S. (actual size)*

The following pages show the great variety of designs used for love brooches. It is a field in which the collector may still do much useful study. A detailed study of hallmarks which reveal dates, makers' initials and assay offices could provide a fascinating line of research for any keen student of sentimental jewellery.

61 (above) *Silver brooch in the shape of an artist's palette decorated with clasped hands, flowers and leaves*
62 (below) *Heart-shaped silver brooch with beaded edge decorated with a basket surmounted by flowers, a butterfly and a love-bird*

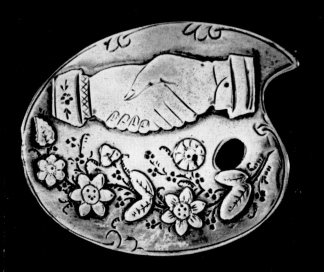

Victorian Symbolism

Flowers, hands, anchors, knots, as well as the more usual heart, were, for the Victorians, symbolic of emotions, attitudes and aspirations, and their significance continued into Edwardian times and beyond.

In 1856 a dictionary of over 700 flowers and their meanings, *The Illustrated Language of Flowers*, was compiled and edited by Mrs L. Burke, and published by A. Routledge & Co. More than fifty years later, in 1913, this little book was copied by a Mr F. W. H. as a handwritten and hand-painted gift to his wife, and this, in turn, was reprinted as a complete facsimile by Michael Joseph in 1968. The following verse is included in the handwritten version:

> There is a language, 'little known',
> Lovers claim it as their own.
> Its symbols smile upon the land
> Wrought by Nature's wondrous hand;
> And in their silent beauty speak
> Of life and joy, to those who seek
> For Love Divine and sunny hours
> In the language of the flowers.
>
> F. W. H.

63 (above) *Silver name brooch with stamped decoration and beaded edge*
64 (below) *Silver bar brooch carrying two love-birds*

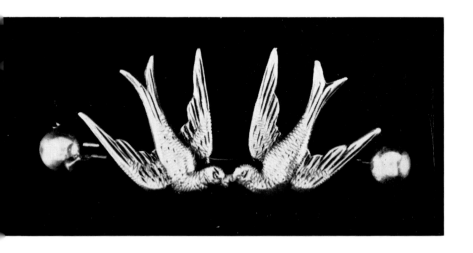

Flowers and leaves were the chief symbols used to decorate Victorian love brooches, though it is not always easy to identify an individual flower or leaf on the stamped out designs. Clover and shamrock, for example, are hard to separate. The following list, however, will be useful particularly for identification of the symbols on enamelled and mourning jewellery where the flowers are less stylised.

65 (above) *Silver name brooch decorated with a heart, leaves and flowers. Assayed in 1900*

66 (below) *Silver name brooch with irregularly scalloped edge, decorated with leaves and flowers. Assayed in 1887*

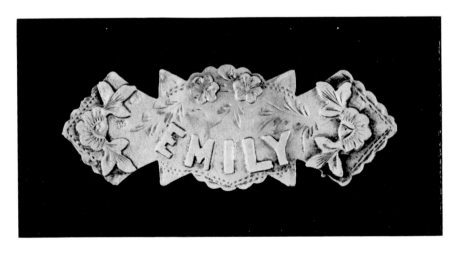

Almond, Flowering . . . Hope
Anemone, garden . . . Forsaken (56)
Balm . . . Sympathy
Bay leaf . . . I change but in death
Bell flower, white . . . Gratitude
Bluebell . . . Constancy
Campanula . . . Gratitude
Carnation, red . . . Alas for my poor heart
China rose . . . Beauty always new
Chrysanthemum . . . I love
Clover, four-leaved . . . Be mine
Clover, white . . . Think of me
Convolvulus, major . . . Extinguished hopes or eternal sleep (22, 72)
Coreopsis, Arkansa . . . Love at first sight
Cuckoo Pint . . . Ardour

67 (above) *Silver brooch in the form of a fan with scalloped edge, decorated with a love-bird. Assayed in 1897*
68 (below) *Silver heart-shaped brooch with beaded edge, decorated with flowers and leaves*

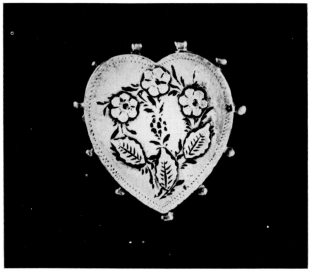

Daffodil . . . Regard
Daisy, garden . . . I share your sentiment
Fern . . . Sincerity (69)
Forget-Me-Not . . . True love (2, 4, 6, 22, 23, 72, 73)
Furze or Gorse . . . Enduring affection
Harebell . . . Grief
Heartsease or Pansy . . . I am always thinking of you
Honesty . . . Sincerity
Honeysuckle . . . Bonds of love
Ivy . . . Friendship, fidelity, marriage. This leaf appears frequently
on love brooches (69, 88, 90, 93, 111, 115)
Jonquil . . . I hope for a return of affection
Lily of the Valley . . . The return of happiness (55)
Marigold . . . Grief or Despair

69 (above) *Silver brooch of twin hearts decorated with a pattern of ivy, fern and leaves*
70 (below) *Silver and enamel book brooch made to slide open*

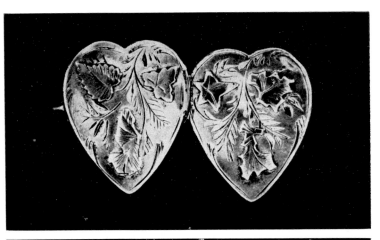

Pears . . . Affection

Poppy, red . . . Consolation

Rose . . . Love (4, 6, 9, 15, 72, 75). There were many varieties of rose; well over thirty had a special meaning. A cabbage rose, for example, was 'an ambassador of love' and a white rose meant 'I am worthy of you'. Such niceties, however, are not relevant when the rose is used as a symbol on jewellery. The rose is sometimes used on commemorative pieces as the symbol for England (75)

Rosemary . . . Remembrance

Sage . . . Domestic virtue

Shamrock . . . Light-heartedness. The shamrock on jewellery is mainly used as the national symbol for Ireland (75), sometimes with an Irish harp (74).

Snowdrop . . . Hope

Star of Bethlehem . . . Purity

Sweet William . . . Gallantry

71 (above) *Silver brooch in the form of a beaded coin wrapped around with a ribbon decorated with shamrock and grasses*

72 (below) *Oval silver brooch with a deep blue enamelled panel decorated with roses, forget-me-nots, shamrock and convolvulus*

Thistle, Scotch . . . Retaliation. The thistle is commonly used as
  a national symbol as on the brooch with clasped hands (73)
  and commemorative brooches (75).
Tulip, red . . . Declaration of love
Violet, blue . . . Faithfulness
Wheat . . . Riches or the continuation of life
White lily . . . Purity and modesty
Willow, weeping . . . Mourning
Yew . . . Sorrow (6)

73 (above) *Oval brooch in silver decorated with clasped hands,
    thistles and chains of flowers. The edge is scalloped and beaded*
74 (below) *Silver brooch carrying the words FORGET-ME-NOT
    in gilt, decorated with gilded harp and shamrocks*

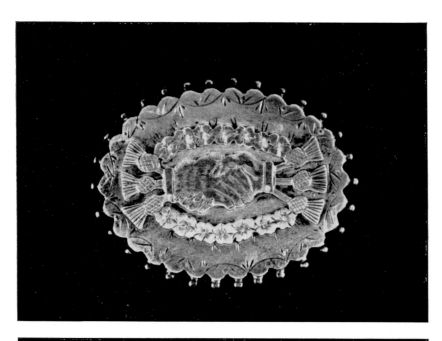

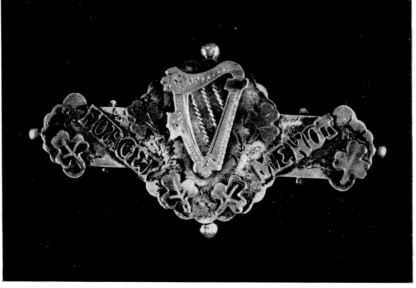

The Silver Jubilee brooch of 1887 (75) uses the rose, shamrock and thistle as national symbols. These are reasonably clearly defined, but it is difficult to identify the flowers on the name brooch (76) with certainty though the central flower may well be the Star of Bethlehem. Five-petalled flowers appear very frequently on love brooches and usually represent the forget-me-not or true love (2, 4, 6, 22, 23, 72, 73). Love-birds are often associated with flowers (77, 93) and sometimes several types of flower are arranged in a woven basket (57, 86, 114).

75 (above) *Heart-shaped silver brooch with beaded edge. A dominant 'V' in gold above the word JUBILEE occupies the centre and is surrounded by thistle, rose and shamrock as an expression of the unity of the kingdom. Assayed in 1887*

76 (below) *Oval silver name brooch with scalloped and beaded edge. The decoration is of flowers and leaves*

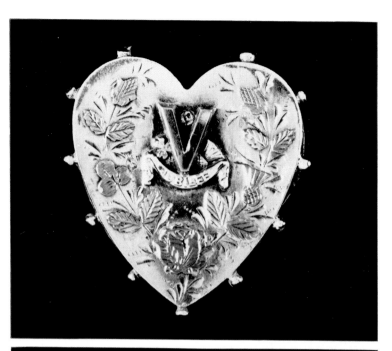

77 (above) *Silver love-bird brooch with decoration of flowers and leaves on a background formed by two crescents*
78 (below) *Gilded twin-heart MIZPAH brooch. The flowers on the left and the rim of the heart on the right are in blue enamel*

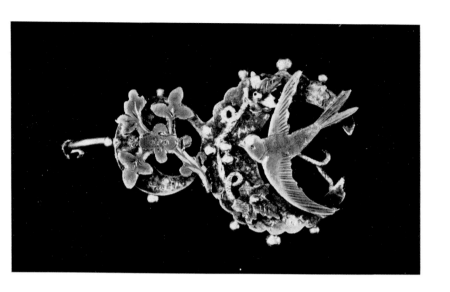

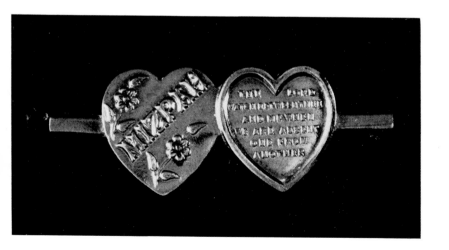

(ii) The Anchor

Many people associate an anchor on jewellery with the sea and assume that a brooch carrying this symbol was given by a sailor to his sweetheart before departing on a long voyage. In fact, the anchor is normally used as a symbol for hope and is often found on mourning jewellery (18, 53) as well as love brooches (79). It is frequently associated with a cross and a heart, the three together symbolic of faith, hope and charity.

79 (above) *Gold brooch with gold bar supporting twin hearts carrying the symbols of faith, hope and charity*
80 (below) *A lovers' knot brooch carrying three amethysts as a centre-piece*

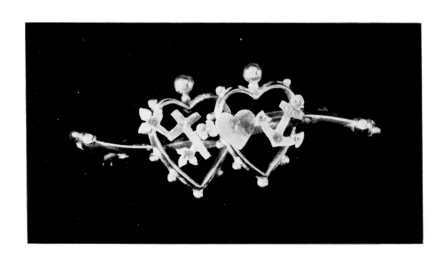

(iii) Coral

Coral is often found on love brooches (81, 82) and intimated warmth and love. Children's gifts were sometimes inlaid with coral—christening rattles, for example.

(iv) The Cross or Crucifix

The cross is seen more frequently on mourning jewellery (7, 18, 19, 20, 53) than on silver brooches (79). It appears most frequently after about 1880, particularly on pieces made in Catholic Ireland. When associated with an anchor and heart it symbolises the virtues of faith, hope and charity.

81   (above) *Silver brooch with parallel bars bearing gilt flowers. The central flower of coral is framed in rococo scrolls and beading*

82   (below) *Silver brooch with a central lozenge filled with coral to represent precious stones. The bar is scalloped and decorated with flowers and leaves*

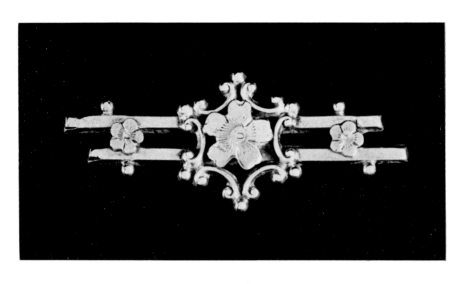

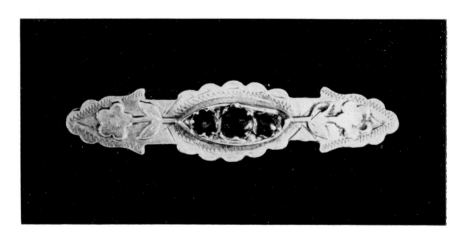

(v) The Hand

A single hand, usually holding a spray or wreath of flowers is frequently seen in mourning jewellery carved from Whitby jet (6). It was worn by a widow or mourner, usually in memory of a husband or sweetheart.

Clasped hands, however, intimate friendship and affection and appear frequently on love brooches (73, 84, 85, 111, 112).

83 (above) *Silver name-brooch with BABY enamelled in blue*
84 (below) *Metal brooch with 'silver' finish showing two female hands clasped in friendship*

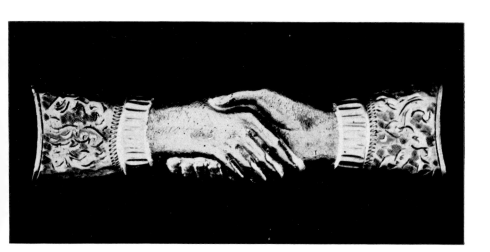

85 (above) *Silver brooch in which two hands hold a heart sur-mounted by a crown. Two shamrock leaves, one in green enamel, provide decoration*

86 (below) *Circular silver brooch decorated with a basket of flowers and leaves. Spaced beading provides a decorative finish*

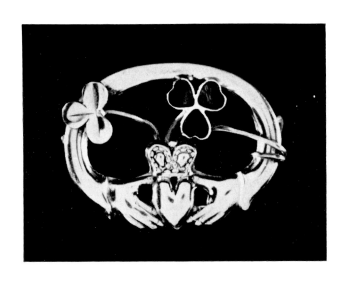

(vi) The Heart

Designers used the heart as a symbol of love and affection. It appears frequently on mourning jewellery (27, 53). On love brooches two hearts are linked (79, 87, 88, 90, 108, 112, 114, 116). Occasionally a heart is surmounted by a crown, presumably indicating that the giver considers the wearer 'queen of my heart' (85).

87 (above) *Heart-shaped silver brooch with scalloped edge, decorated with a horseshoe, leaves and flowers. Assayed in 1894* $(\times 1\frac{1}{2})$

88 (below) *Brooch with two silver hearts, the upper outlines reversed, linked by a gilded MIZPAH flanked by gilded ivy leaves. The smaller flowers are alternately silver and gilt*

89　(above) *Silver brooch with fern and flower motifs and a central heart*

90　(below) *Silver brooch with two hearts shot through by an arrow. A small central heart, flowers and ivy leaves are superimposed in gilt. Assayed in 1894*

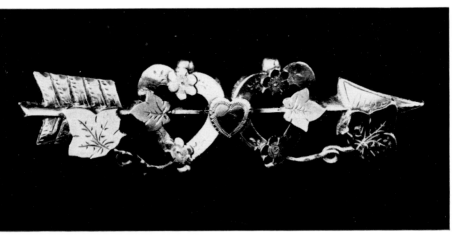

(vii) *The Horseshoe*

The horseshoes on love brooches are for 'good fortune' and are usually inverted (87, 91, 102, 107). Apparently the country superstition about the loss of luck from an inverted shoe did not concern the wearers.

(viii) *Lovers' Knots*

These are intended to secure the bonds of love, fidelity and friendship (80, 110). A variant of the lovers' knot is the buckle (94).

91 (above) *Silver brooch with scalloped edge, decorated with horseshoe, flowers and leaves*
92 (below) *Rectangular silver brooch decorated with an infant's wicker cradle to mark a new arrival in the family. A space has been left in the bottom left-hand corner so that the baby's name may be engraved later*

93 (above) *Silver brooch with a central pair of love-birds flanked by flowers and ivy leaves. The edge of the brooch is scalloped. Assayed in 1889* ($\times$ $1\frac{1}{2}$)

94 (below) *Silver buckle with clasp on a belt design with a border of flowers and leaves, the edge decorated with spaced beading*

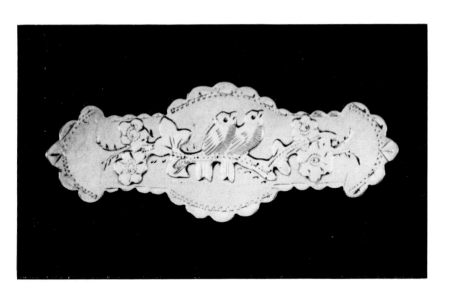

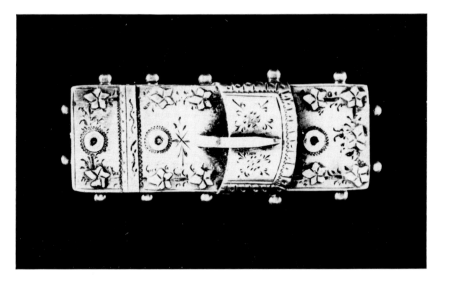

(ix) *Pearls*

Pearls are used on mourning jewellery as symbols of tears (22, 44).

(x) *The Serpent*

The serpent appears frequently on mourning jewellery (8, 16). It was made popular by Queen Victoria whose engagement ring was in the form of a serpent.

95 (above) *Silver brooch with twisted ribbon design*
96 (below) *Small silver name brooch, the letters decorated with seed pearls* ($\times$ 3)

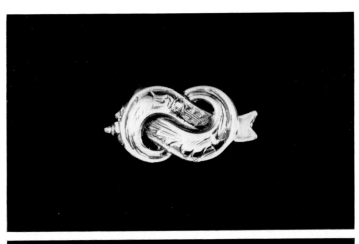

(xi) Unusual Symbolism

The love brooch in the form of a visiting card with one corner turned over (98) is puzzling. One can only quote from an etiquette book of the period:

> Should the lady upon whom you call not be at home, you may turn down one corner of the card, to signify that you have called personally, but this is variously interpreted, sometimes that the card has been left also for the daughters of the house, or that the mother who called has been accompanied by her daughter.

Occasionally a symbol of a leisure occupation is included in a brooch—a palette (61), a stringed instrument (99) or a harp (100).

97 (above) *Circular name brooch with beaded edge*
98 (below) *Rectangular silver name brooch with beaded edge in the form of a visiting card with corner turned down. Decoration is of flowers and leaves*

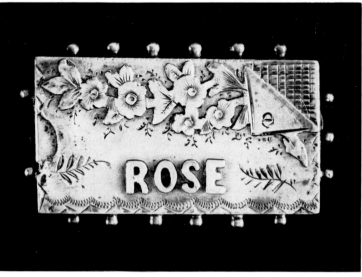

99 (above) *Crescent-shaped silver brooch decorated with beading, flowers and a stringed instrument, the whole mounted on a stave which carries the pin*

100 (below) *Heavy silver harp brooch with twisted silver wire to represent the strings*

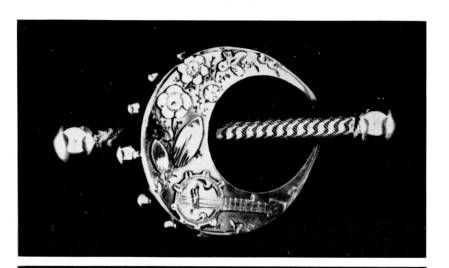

Name Brooches

Name brooches were undoubtedly produced in large quantities in late Victorian times but nevertheless show some individuality (59, 63, 65, 66, 76, 97, 98, 101, 104, 106, 109). It is very rare indeed to find two exactly alike. Personal research has never yet been able to match two as an example of early mass production. Any collection of name brooches will reflect the popularity of girls' names in Victorian days—Alice, Ann, Dora, Emily, Florence, Ida, Jennie, Lucy, Nellie, Nina, Rose, Susan and Winnie, occur fairly frequently. Such brooches were commonly given as presents in working-class families. Indeed they were used to express affection between members of the family. There are brooches which simply say 'Mother' (103) or 'Baby' (83). If the name of a baby was not known when the brooch was sold, it would be engraved later. The brooch with a cradle (92) shows a space left for this purpose.

101 (above) *Circular silver name brooch with beaded cog-shaped border. Leaves fill the circle above and below the name which has punched decoration. Assayed in 1881*

102 (below) *Scalloped silver brooch decorated with flowers and leaves. A central horseshoe holds a rose in white and pink enamel*

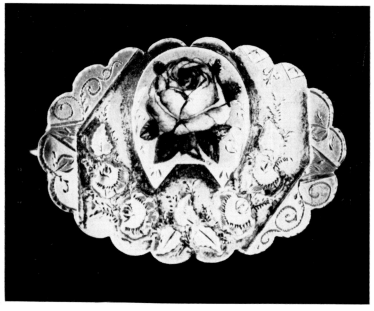

103 (above) *Name brooch with the silvered word MOTHER on a base of mock ivory* ($\times$ $1\frac{1}{2}$)

104 (below) *Silver name brooch with stamped decoration. Assayed in 1894* ($\times$ $1\frac{1}{2}$)

105 (above) *Heart-shaped silver brooch with cusped and beaded border in the Gothic taste, engraved with the initial 'C'*

106 (below) *Oval name brooch of silver with decorative beaded border, the name held by sprays of flowers and leaves*

H

Message Brooches

Some brooches carry a message (107, 110). The commonest type is the Mizpah brooch (78, 88, 108), given when lovers were likely to be parted for a considerable period. These usually consisted of twin hearts united and often carried the Old Testament text (Genesis 31:49) in full:

> And Mizpah; for he said, The Lord watch between me and thee, when we are absent one from another.

107 (above) *Silver horseshoe message brooch with scalloped edge*
108 (below) *Silver Mizpah brooch of twin hearts with beaded edges, decorated with flowers and leaves*

109 (above) *Lozenge-shaped silver name brooch with beaded edge, decorated with leaves and flowers*

110 (below) *Silver message brooch with a centrepiece of two hearts linked by a bow tied as a lover's knot. Decoration includes flowers and leaves*

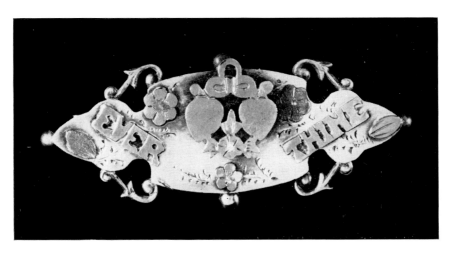

111 (above) *Silver message brooch with clasped hands, ivy leaves, and a scroll with the words SEASON'S GREETINGS*

112 (below) *Silver brooch with a centrepiece of two hands clasped through joined hearts, decorated with ivy leaves, flowers and beading*

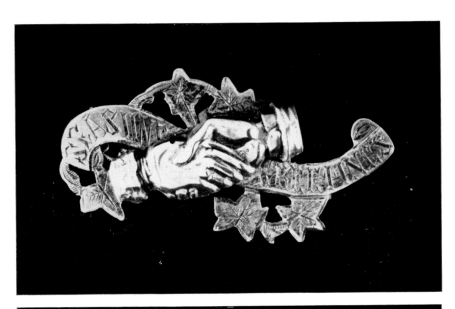

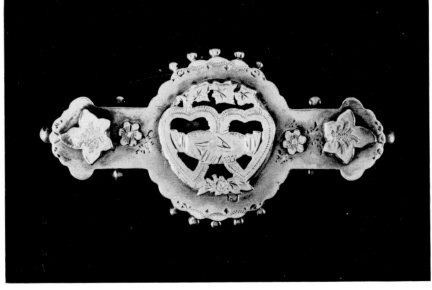

Personal Mementoes

The use of hair in mourning jewellery has already been discussed. It was occasionally used in lockets, when lovers were parted, as a memento of the absent lover. More usually, however, a love brooch was adapted to carry a photograph (58, 113).

113 (above) *Gilt frame brooch with beaded edge made to carry a photograph*

114 (below) *Silver brooch in which two hearts are joined by a twisted bar which carries a central bow from which hangs a basket of flowers*

Commemorative Brooches

A few love brooches in silver were made to commemorate the Silver Jubilee of 1887, but by 1897 the love brooch had fully established itself as the most popular item of sentimental jewellery, and many were produced to mark the occasion of the Diamond Jubilee. They often carry two hearts as well as 'VR' and a crown (116). Many also carry the dates '1837–1897' to mark the 'sixty glorious years'.

115 (above) *Silver brooch decorated with a bow and ivy leaves. Small beads of silver add sparkle to the outline. Assayed in 1888*

116 (below) *Silver brooch made to mark the Diamond Jubilee of Queen Victoria, carrying the letters 'VR' surmounted by a crown. Below are the dates 1837–97 representing the 'sixty glorious years'. The two hearts made it both a love brooch and a commemorative item of jewellery. Assayed in 1897*

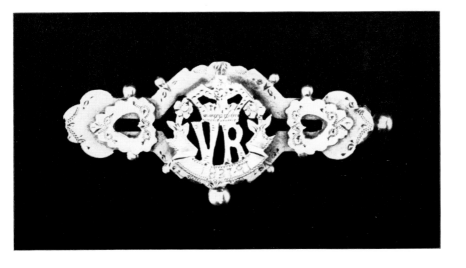

Bibliography

Bedford, J. *Jewellery* (1964)

Bendon, K. *Ornament and Jewellery* (1967)

Bradford, E. *English Victorian Jewellery* (1959, 1967)
    Four Centuries of European Jewellery (1953, 1967)

Burgess, E. *Antique Jewellery and Trinkets* (1919)

Castellani, A. *Antique Jewellery and its Revival* (1862)

Curran, A. *Collecting Jewellery* (1963)
    Jewels and Gems (1961)

Evans, J. *A History of Jewellery, 1100–1870* (1953, 1970)

Flower, M. *Victorian Jewellery* (1951, revised 1967)
    Jewellery, 1837–1901 (1968)

Hinks, P. *Jewellery* (1969)

Kendall, H. P. *The Story of Whitby Jet* (Whitby, 1936)

Laver, J. *Victoriana* (1966)

Prosser, W. *Birmingham Inventions* (1881)

Wood, V. *Victoriana: A Collector's Guide* (1960, 1968)

Acknowledgements

We would like to thank all those who have given us their expert help and advice in the preparation of this book, particularly: Simeon Gorlof of Hatton Garden and Kensington High Street, London; Hope & Eleanor of the Chelsea Antique Market, London, for the loan of a number of brooches; the Librarian of the Guildhall Library, London, for allowing us to see 'The History, Development and Organisation of the Birmingham Jewellery and Allied Trades' by J..C. Roche, an unpublished thesis presented for the degree of Master of Commerce, University of Birmingham, 1927; the Chief Librarian, Whitby Public Library; the Custodian of Jewellery, Victoria and Albert Museum and London Museum; and the Curators of the Science Museum and Geological Museum, London.

Photography by Maillard Studio, London.